I'M NO LONGER THE WEIRD ONE IN THE ROOM

"THIS BOOK IS A MUST-READ for people starting on their spiritual path, and for those who have been on the path, it's a reminder of how far we've come. Each essay is filled with inspiring ideas and personal truths as it beautifully leads the reader into the author's amazing journey of self-discovery and becoming more fully human. I loved this book! Thank you for writing it!"

—*Julie Russell, RN, LRMT, CHt, CC, ICRT Senior Licensed Reiki Master Teacher, Integrative Medicine Practitioner-Teacher*

"A COMFORTING AND EMPOWERING invitation to trust your spiritual experiences and remember who you truly are. This book is a warm and reassuring companion for anyone awakening to their spiritual self."

—*Kerry Jehanne-Guadalupe, author of THRESHOLDS OF BECOMING: THE ALCHEMY OF BEING—INDIVIDUAL AND COLLECTIVE*

"A SIMPLE AND EASY-TO-FOLLOW GUIDE for becoming aware of and appreciating the daily miracles of life."

—*Bodhi Starwater, author of 5 ELEMENTS OF SOUND HEALING*

"WHETHER YOUR JOURNEY IS JUST BEGINNING or already unfolding, this book offers a thoughtful reminder to recognize and appreciate the path the Divine continues to reveal. Through personal experiences and meaningful insight, Shine Redwood gently guides you back to the essence of your Divine Self."

—*John Nap*, *author of* GALACTIC AWAKENING: A COSMIC JOURNEY OF REMEMBRANCE, INTEGRATION, AND ASCENSION

"I LOVED THESE SHORT STORIES. Shine writes in a way that is simple, clear, and accessible. Perfect for beginners, and also a beautiful reminder for those already on a Spiritual Path."

—*Shari M. Carolo*, *The Stargate Experience Facilitator and Community Leader, Sacramento*

I'M NO LONGER THE WEIRD ONE IN THE ROOM

AND NEITHER ARE YOU. IT'S OKAY TO TALK ABOUT YOUR SPIRITUAL EXPERIENCES.

SHINE REDWOOD

818
ARCTURUS

I'm No Longer the Weird One in the Room

And neither are you. It's okay to talk about your spiritual experiences.

Copyright © 2026 by Shine Redwood

Published by 818 Arcturus, Sacramento, California

Cover design by 818 Arcturus, Sacramento, California

Library of Congress Control Number: 2026906268

ISBN: 978-0-9860983-6-9 (paperback)

ISBN: 978-0-9860983-9-0 (ebook)

Excerpt found in Coincidence? Never: *Listening in With Eckhart Tolle*, Unity Magazine (unitymagazine.org), November/December 2015, page 27.

Excerpt found in The Power of Spiritual Maturity: *Diana Coopers Words of Wisdom: June 2025*, The Portugal News (theportugalnews.com), May 28, 2025.

GETTING STARTED

Dear friend,

I'M NO LONGER THE WEIRD ONE IN THE ROOM is a series of short essays that I felt compelled to write from January 2025 to July 2025. I encourage you to let intuition guide you through the content. Begin by asking yourself: *What do I need to read now?* Then scan the table of contents until a title grabs your attention. That's where you should start.

Shine Redwood

February 2026

CONTENTS

INTRODUCTION

One of the most important tasks we can do in our lifetime is share our life experiences. As the storyteller, it's a beautiful way to heal and learn. As the receiver, we are introduced to perspectives we may not have considered.

Ancient communities relied on stories to improve their way of life and expand their thinking. Survival would have been difficult without this practice. We need to remember that our experiences are powerful. They all matter. And they should be shared.

The ideas in these essays come from direct experience, intuition, meditation, reading, and talking to people about their experiences.

My goal is not to change your mind about these topics but to inspire you to be curious, so you feel comfortable with exploring a topic on your own.

Like anything, you may or may not resonate with all of the content. That's okay. We are constantly changing and evolving. What doesn't resonate with you now may resonate with you next year. That's how life works. Focus on what feels true to you right now.

Enjoy the journey.

"Not all those who wander are lost."
— J.R.R. Tolkien

There comes a point in everyone's life when they accept that there is more to this world, this life, than what we see with our human eyes.

Our senses, like an antenna, pick up frequencies that we can feel but we can't see.

That's when we start to pay attention . . . because a coincidence feels like a personal message, and a dream feels so real it's all-consuming.

COINCIDENCE? NEVER

NUDGES FROM THE UNIVERSE
LET US KNOW THAT WE ARE
ALWAYS BEING SUPPORTED.

ABOUT THOSE COINCIDENCES YOU'RE noticing ... Are you still ignoring them?

It's time to take a closer look at their meaning.

I've been paying attention to "coincidences" for decades.

Once you understand why they keep occurring, you realize how magical they are.

Every subtle "coincidence" is an *offer of support* from the universe (for you, this might be your higher self, loved ones who have transitioned, angels, God, ancestors, or galactic family).

You have the option to accept the support or ignore it. It's your free will.

I've learned that accepting the support helps create a smooth flow in my life.

Here's an excellent example of how it works ... In the movie *City of Angels,* there's a scene where an air traffic controller is distracted by thoughts of his personal life; he's not paying attention to the flight screen in front of him.

Just before the possibility of a mid-air disaster, he is jolted out of his thoughts and gives instructions to the pilots.

Behind him the whole time is an angel who gently touches his shoulder at the right moment and jolts his mind back to the task in front of him. (Don't you love it when the movie industry sneaks a spiritual secret into a script?)

We've all had a similar experience. How many times have you been jolted to attention while driving a car?

I once saw a car in front of me, heading straight for a wall at high speed, change direction just moments before the crash. Not only was I screaming at him, but I also imagined an angel or ancestor screaming at him to turn the wheel. I'm glad he felt the message.

There are no accidents. No coincidences. No bad luck or good luck. It's all goodness for our growth and expansion.

We are forces of nature, creating everything around us with our energy.

And the universe likes to play along by offering support when we ask for it.

I enjoy playing with the energy, having fun with it, and am always truly grateful for the support.

Here's another great example … Eckhart Tolle was recently interviewed about the first book to be featured in his new imprint, An Eckhart Tolle Edition, with New World Library.

It was no coincidence that this parenting book belonged in his new imprint.

He explains why: "It emerged as the first book through a series of synchronistic events — including meeting the author a couple of times and discovering strange synchronistic connections between us, and then learning that she was writing a book at the time. That was a clear message. I always pay attention to synchronicities."

He continues: "I always listen for messages through synchronistic events or chance encounters. Most humans are so absorbed in their thinking that there's not much attention left for perceiving the miraculous universe around them at every moment. They don't have the wakefulness necessary to listen to messages coming from outside or promptings coming from within, such as intuitive realizations and creative insights. Spiritual awakening involves stepping out of that complete absorption in your thought processes so that you can become aware and present, and then living from that level."

These special moments are all around us every day, offering inspiration, support, and guidance.

The universe's nudges are its way of letting us know that we are always being supported.

Know this. Feel it. Accept the support.

I'M NO LONGER THE WEIRD ONE IN THE ROOM

AND NEITHER ARE YOU. IT'S OKAY TO TALK ABOUT YOUR SPIRITUAL EXPERIENCES.

I CAN'T BELIEVE IT.

No longer am I the weird one in the room.

People today ask me questions about my metaphysical ideas, and nine times out of ten, they want to share their own experiences.

To be honest, I didn't think I'd ever see masses of people open their minds and be honest about their experiences, not in this lifetime.

But here it is.

It's exciting!

Most of us have been conditioned since birth to fear and deny anything unfamiliar. This never made sense to me.

No one person has all the knowledge of the universe.

If I'm not curious and open and ask questions, how will I understand the universe?

Knowledge can't hurt you, unless you twist it into something harmful.

My understanding of the world and the universe is constantly changing because I'm constantly getting new knowledge.

A topic I thought I understood when I was 21 years old has evolved; it has been upgraded.

How information *feels* is the key.

I listen, then observe how the information feels in my body.

If it feels right (in the moment) or resonates with me, I let it be (neutral).

If it doesn't feel right, the information isn't for me, and I move on.

If I feel fear or anger, I ask myself why. The reason is always the result of old conditioning that I haven't let go of.

I believe we exist to share our knowledge and experiences because every life is unique and contributes to the whole of everything.

As far back as I can remember, I have been a curious soul.

Are people the same everywhere?

What drives them to do what they do?

Who am I in this mix?

Why am I here?

What's the purpose of it all?

In my free time, I like to learn, explore, and experience the mysteries of the world, including spiritual metaphysics topics such as divination, telepathy, reincarnation, tarot, dowsing, energy healing, spirit guides and angels, and communicating with those who have left Earth.

This has been an obsession of mine for more than 50 years, and I've learned that human life on Earth is as fascinating as it is complex.

For the first time, in short essays, I will share my personal experiences. Stay with me, and please share your thoughts and experiences.

WHY LIFE ON EARTH
IS SO IMPORTANT

EVERY ONCE IN A WHILE, I COME ACROSS A universal truth that resonates with me so strongly it changes my understanding of why life on Earth is so important.

Not long ago, I heard a truth that stopped me in my tracks, and I haven't been able to stop thinking about it.

I'm referring to how important *life experiences* are and the role they play in a person's soul growth.

This idea may seem simple, even obvious, but it is also essential to understand that a person's consciousness *purposely* creates these experiences.

Some experiences feel good. Some experiences don't feel good. Both scenarios benefit the soul by providing an opportunity to mature and grow.

What if you had to choose from hearing a story about an experience, watching a video of someone having an experience, or having the experience yourself? What would you choose?

The popular option for most souls is to have a direct experience so it's possible to touch, smell, hear, and feel every emotional aspect of the experience.

This is where the magic happens — where the soul makes the biggest leap into maturity.

How does it feel to lose everything? If I murdered someone and spent my adult life in jail, what would that do to my soul? I've never been a woman who lived in Japan; what would that be like? How would my soul expand if I were a man who was happily married for 51 years? What if I were surrounded by racism? How would that experience change who I am? What if I lost my parents when I was six years old? What if I died in a war?

Your consciousness chooses every experience. In this lifetime. And every lifetime your soul has ever planned.

WHEN THINGS GET HARD, REMEMBER:

The purpose of every experience — big, small, mundane — is to help your soul expand.

Pause a moment and remember this when you're having an experience that pains you.

Your soul needs to have the experience.

Allow yourself to feel every aspect of it.

In time, you will begin to move through the emotion of the experience.

Then you will sense a bubble of peace and calmness around you, a byproduct of understanding and acceptance.

There may be years when it feels like a particular experience is on repeat. This is on purpose.

Eventually, your soul will master the challenge, and it will stop showing up in your life or become much easier for you to manage.

Your soul knew you were strong enough to get through the hard moments.

It also knew that you would be surrounded by helpers and guides in spirit. They are there now, willing to help. Just ask.

THE SUMMER I RECONNECTED WITH MY SPIRITUAL SELF

A SIMPLE ACTIVITY EVERY DAY HELPED ME ESTABLISH A DAILY ROUTINE.

DURING THE SUMMER OF 2022, I MADE A commitment to spend more time with my spiritual self.

I've always been connected to that part of me, but in early 2022, the connection was on the sideline, playing a much smaller part than my work/career self.

My life needed a rebalance. I could feel it.

But this meant pulling back on my work/career, and that's not always easy. I reassured myself that the adjustment would be just a few months. No big deal. Eventually, those few months turned into a year. That's how much I enjoyed a more balanced life.

I started slow, incorporating one new activity into my daily routine.

Taking on too many activities would have knocked my life out of balance again.

I let my intuition select the activity.

Every day, I asked myself, *What feels right today?* Some days it was one activity. Other days, it was more than one, like a 10-minute morning meditation, a yoga class, and a nightly gratitude moment.

Here are the nine activities I indulged in:

Meditation and mindfulness

- Meditation helped me quiet my mind, elevate my intuition, and deepen my spiritual connection to self.
- Mindfulness encouraged me to be fully present and appreciate every moment.

Grounding

- To ground myself, I spent time in nature … walking, exploring, hiking, and gardening.
- These peaceful moments pulled me away from everything in my world and helped me connect with planet Earth.

Reading and learning

- I explored spiritual teachings that were new to me (videos, writings, books) to broaden my book of knowledge.

- Once I found topics that resonated with me, I searched for teachings that deepened my understanding.

JOURNALING AND SELF-REFLECTION

- I wrote down my thoughts and spiritual insights when they appeared.
- I reflected on personal beliefs — how they changed or stayed the same — as my spiritual awareness evolved.

SPIRITUAL COMMUNITIES

- I joined various spiritual groups in my area (Reiki circle, meditation group, drum circle) to meet like-minded people.
- Not only did I gain new friendships, but some of us gathered outside of the groups to discuss spiritual topics.

ACTS OF KINDNESS

- I wanted to help others with my actions, not my wallet. So I volunteered at local food banks, including one that had a large garden that needed tending.
- When I left the house, I practiced compassion for others. I smiled at a stranger. I gave a

friendly wave to the driver who cut in front of me. I said a kind word to the person who looked like they were not having a good day.

BREATHWORK AND YOGA

- I signed up for an all-day class to learn breathwork and incorporated it into Reiki and other energy healing modalities.
- I joined a yoga studio for one year to learn how to align my body, mind, and spirit.

GRATITUDE AND AFFIRMATIONS

- I practiced gratitude every morning and every night before I fell asleep.
- Affirmations helped me reinforce my spiritual beliefs.

CREATIVE EXPRESSION

- Music, dance, and writing are my creative outlets. These activities are a gift to myself, allowing me to express myself and connect with my emotions.
- Creative activities and walking in nature are a form of meditation for me.

Some of these activities only take a few minutes. Try incorporating them into your daily life for seven days. You'll feel the difference they make, and you'll fall into a habit that takes very little effort.

If you're easily bored with routines, switch to a new activity every day. Whatever works for you is the right fit.

> **"What you are looking for is what is looking."**
> — St. Francis of Assisi

It's critical that we remember how powerful we are.

We are all creators, capable of creating a life we want, not a life society has forced us to accept.

We even have a superpower . . . intuition. It warns us of danger when we're in unfamiliar territory, it pokes us when we meet a threatening person, it knows our true self, and it will never mislead us.

BE YOU — THE
WORLD WILL ADJUST

AN INSPIRING LIFE LESSON FROM A TREE.

I HAVE A NATIVE AUSTRALIAN TREE IN MY yard. I named her Sydney.

While Sydney has lived her whole life in northern California, she has memories of her Australian roots.

When the northern hemisphere (California, where she lives) is experiencing spring, the southern hemisphere (Australia, where she's from) is experiencing autumn.

Every year, I watch her transform with the seasons, but not in the same way as the trees around her.

In the winter, when we get rain, fog, and cold temperatures, Sydney is the only tree in the courtyard with ALL her leaves.

She thinks it's summer.

This makes her very popular with the birds.

When the season changes in northern California from spring to summer, Sydney is transitioning from autumn to winter.

Her leaves turn orange, yellow, and red, and by the end of April, there's a carpet of leaves on the grass under her wide canopy.

Meanwhile, the trees around her are developing and expanding new leaves and getting ready for summer.

She's fascinating to watch.

But most of all, I admire her for being true to who she is on the inside, no matter what's going on around her.

Sydney is always Sydney, and the animals and people around her love her just the way she is.

Her message to us . . . In the chaos, as the old completes its collapse and the new is taking form, be your true self.

The world *will* adjust.

ABSOLUTE KNOWING — YOUR SECRET PSYCHIC ABILITY

IF YOU ARE MEANT TO KNOW SOMETHING, YOU WILL KNOW IT.

ABSOLUTE KNOWING IS ONE OF YOUR INNATE psychic abilities.

Yes, you have it. Everyone has it.

The question is, are you using it?

Absolute knowing is one of the psychic "Clairs" referred to as claircognizance. It's when you experience an inner knowing that just pops into your mind.

Think about when you *knew* something was right.

It wasn't something you processed in your mind, or you thought about; it was **a feeling of absolute knowing in your body.**

Maybe it was a new job offer. Or a decision to move to another city. Or an invitation to attend an event. Or a knowing that the money you needed would come.

You didn't question the knowing, and you didn't need proof that it was right.

It was simply a subtle cue, a frequency, that you (your energy field) recognized as trustworthy and truthful.

Your higher self, who cares for you and would never betray you, shared the knowledge, and you felt it in your body.

Absolute or inner knowing can slide in from nowhere at any time.

If you were meant to know something, you will know it.

It may be knowledge to help you with a big life event, or it may be about a small, everyday event.

In both cases, the knowledge is energy — an energetic frequency, a signal — sent from your higher self.

I've experienced many moments of absolute knowing.

A few examples are when I received a nudge from my brother and grandfather after they passed.

My instant interpretation of these nudges was absolute knowing.

Another example was when I visited London for the first time (in this lifetime).

As I explored the city, I *knew* I had lived there in a past life. I knew the streets, I knew my way around, and I felt very comfortable there.

ABSOLUTE KNOWING IS VERY similar to intuition, but I now know it's different.

Absolute knowing is more direct, and there is no question that the knowledge is right or true.

Intuition, on the other hand, is less direct, and if I allow it, my ego can talk me out of an intuitive hit.

However, **my ego *cannot* talk me out of a feeling of absolute knowing**.

Likewise, the knowledge received is not a judgmental thought in your head.

It's a feeling.

A sense of knowing that something is true.

The mind is not involved at all.

I USE both absolute knowing and intuition now more than ever because our world is changing at lightning speed.

This knowledge helps me discern what is happening around me and the people I come in contact with.

I also pay attention to déjà vu moments and make an effort to understand what the experience is trying to help me remember.

But it only happens when I connect with my spiritual self in some way (every day), and I keep my vibrational state high.

It's then that my channel is open to receive support from the universe, whether it comes from my higher self, my angels and guides, or source.

YOUR LIFE'S PURPOSE

A GENTLE REMINDER TO YOUR SPIRIT.

YOU, MY FRIEND, COME FROM SUPERIOR galactic intelligence. You are magnificent in every way.

Your ability to manifest and create your life in any way you wish, using your thoughts, feelings, and emotions, is more impressive than you were taught.

Bit by bit, you will remember the power of your free will and why you are here now.

Never dim your light for anyone or anything. It's why you are here. You were meant to share that light with the world.

What is the purpose of your life, you ask? Your purpose was intentionally designed to reveal itself one layer at a time. Not all at once. That would not serve your spirit.

Be determined to follow your bliss. For now, that's your purpose.

It's not a role or position you occupy, like a parent, engineer, teacher, nurse, police officer, etc. It's so much simpler than what the mind thinks it should be.

What qualities are exclusive to you that open your heart and allow you to bring love into the world? For now, that's your purpose.

What brings you joy? What do you do really well? How do you share your skills and joy with other people? For now, that's your purpose.

We are all here at this moment to allow our spirit to express its individual self, to spread love wherever we go, and to engage in experiences that are unique to our spirit — all while living on beautiful planet Earth.

It is so.

CREATING MOMENTS
THAT RECONNECT YOU
TO YOUR ESSENCE

WHAT MAKES YOU SOAR?

INSIDE YOU IS AN ESSENCE THAT IS UNIQUE to you.

No other being or living thing in all the multiverses has your essence.

Just you.

Only you.

And, wow, the stories your essence could tell.

It's been everything and everywhere it has ever desired.

In your human body, you can't see it or smell it. But you can feel it.

It feels like gentle ocean waves hitting the shore.

In other words, it's calm and natural.

You will also feel it when you're in the zone.

The zone is that space you're in when time stands still, when you look up and hours have gone by.

Wouldn't it be nice to be there more often?

It's possible.

Go there by creating tiny moments throughout the day that connect you to your essence or spirit.

DURING THE DAY:

- Bless your food before you eat.
- Ask the water you drink and the air you breathe to be clear of toxins.
- Place a small Tibetan bell in your car; ring it gently when you're stopped in traffic.
- Fill a small spray bottle with water or carrier oil and a few drops of your favorite essential oil(s); spritz the air around your body.
- When you're in a public place, be kind and remember who you are — a unique essence.
- Place a quartz crystal or a feather in a room where you spend a lot of time; think of the beauty of nature when it catches your eye.
- Be thankful — for the sun, for green stoplights on a long stretch of road, for the perfect parking spot, and more.
- Ask for what you want — good health, to be surrounded by kind people, and so much more.

There are endless ways to surround yourself with items, smells, and sounds that pull you out of the busyness of the day and into the gentle waves of your essence.

BEFORE YOU GO TO SLEEP:

- Look at yourself in a mirror and say, *I love you.*
- Close your eyes and say, *Thank you,* to your essence or spirit and to your guides and helpers for another day on Earth.
- Ask for what you want — restful sleep, to remember your dreams, healing while you sleep, anything.

Your essence is a natural creator.

Let it create the life you want to live.

PHASE III - LEARNING TO STAY GROUNDED

"You do not have to be calm to be centered."
— Jack Kornfield

The human body was not designed to live in a messy world.

And it's becoming too much — toxins in our food and air, electromagnetic fields that disturb our body's electrical system, and emotional distress caused by long periods of feeling divided and distant from each other.

Our whole self is screaming for more balance.

CALMING AND RESTORING
THE NERVOUS SYSTEM

5 SIMPLE WAYS I RESET
MY BRAIN AND ENERGY.

𝕎 TODAY I NEED SUNSHINE. IT'S STILL SPRING, and mornings are beautiful where I live, so I find a bench that's drenched in morning sun. I'm comfortable, my eyes are closed, and the sun's healing rays are energizing the cells in my body. I stay in this space for as long as I need. There's no rush. About 10 minutes feels right.

𝕎 On the full moon, I joined a group of spiritually minded people for an evening drum circle. Every drum and beat had something enlightening to share. I was transformed into a dreamlike state, with eyes closed, as I absorbed the rhythmic sound of the drums and the vibration of my own drum. Suddenly, I can breathe deeply again, and I'm more aware of the calmness in my body. About 30 minutes have passed.

I stop and observe the tension in my body when I feel stressed. By observing what's happening — versus being in the stress — I can do something to change how my body feels. I pause and observe my breath until I sense a place of calm.

W Today I need to feel the energy of the 100+ year-old oak tree in the park. I sense it knows I'm coming before I cross the footbridge in its direction. I begin to breathe deeply. I see it in the distance. Its canopy is perfectly shaped regardless of the season. I place the palms of my hands on its trunk, close my eyes, and we exchange energy. There's no rush. About 8 minutes fly by.

W At this moment, I need to be calm. I turn my attention to my breath. I take a deeeeep breath in (all the way down to my belly), hold it for a few seconds, and then push it down my body and through the bottoms of my feet. I do this again and a third time. I am calm. About 2 minutes pass.

I consistently practice calming my nervous system. My goal is to stay centered and glide through chaos.

W Today I'm too much in my head; I need to be grounded in my body. I stand and bend to touch my toes, repeating this movement five times. Then I lock my feet, legs, and hips firmly in place and twist my upper body and spine to the left and then to the right, repeating this movement ten times. The electrical energy in my body is flowing again. This clears my head and wakes up my body. About 3 minutes slip away.

IT'S NOT EASY —
BUT IT'S WORTH IT

A BALANCED LIFE IS MORE
IMPORTANT THAN EVER.

I DON'T LIKE HOW IMBALANCE *FEELS*, WHETHER it's in my body, mind, or spirit.

It feels like something is off, and it is.

The frequency of whatever is causing the imbalance does not match my frequency.

I've also noticed that I'm much more conscious of that feeling.

But why? Why do I need to create a state of balance within and around me? Why am I more conscious of imbalance?

Because when I'm balanced, life is softer. It's less work. It flows. It *feels* beautiful.

A BALANCED BODY WITH MOVEMENT, DIET, AND SUPPLEMENTS

Movement is a critical component of a balanced body.

When the body moves, energy flows, and that means the body's energy systems are able to push stuck or sluggish energy out of the organs, muscles, and other parts of the body.

Even minor, consistent movement throughout the day helps keep the body's energy balanced.

Physical movement in variation also helps maintain balance.

On Monday, a long walk is appealing, on Thursday, your body wants to run, and a week later, it wants to stretch in a gentle way with yoga.

Listening to the body, quietly asking it what it needs, ensures it is not pushed too hard, and it gets what it needs on the day it needs it.

If you forget to listen and push too hard, the body will let you know.

The quality of the body's fuel is certain — it needs fresh, organic food and water to stay in a balanced state.

And similar to daily movement, it prefers a variety of foods instead of the same food every day.

Variation ensures it receives a mix of vitamins and minerals and allows the gut to metabolize different types of food, keeping it strong.

Nutritional supplements are needed because food alone will not provide the body with what it needs to be healthy.

More than a hundred years ago, our soil had nutrients, and our farming practices focused on caring for the land and animals.

Today, our soil is depleted of nutrients, and our water and air are polluted.

High-quality supplements give the body a fighting chance to maintain balance.

What does your body feel like when it's out of balance?

The first sign will be subtle.

Maybe you are more tired than usual. Maybe it's a new ache in the body.

Being aware of a sign as soon as it shows up and making an adjustment allows the body to balance itself more quickly.

Balance is an ongoing practice. But once you get used to it, it gets easier, and it's worth it.

A BALANCED MIND STARTS WITH AWARENESS

Two things are required to maintain balance: 1) awareness and 2) being in the moment.

Being aware of an imbalance happens before anything else.

Once you are aware, can you stay with it?

There is power in that moment.

There is power in sitting with yourself, observing, and feeling a feeling or an emotion.

When you close your eyes and inhale/exhale a few deep breaths, can you find your way through it?

Excess emotion, overthinking, and obsession are all signs of the mind being out of balance.

This includes overreacting to someone's comment or action, a signal that something triggered you, and healing is needed.

If you interact with people and their emotions all day, you may need to clear your emotional energy field more often.

Grounding is a great way to release and clear unwanted energy.

Move your body.

Put your hands in the garden.

Walk in nature.

Sit on the grass.

Take a warm bath with bath salts.

Play with your dog or kids.

Cook.

Watch a movie that makes you laugh.

Drink fresh water.

The key is to catch yourself when you are moving out of balance.

Then you can fix it in the moment.

If you wait until the weekend, your mind will be overloaded, and your efforts won't be as effective.

Do a little every time you see the signs.

A BALANCED SPIRIT IS A FREQUENCY YOU CARRY WITH YOU

Trust is a BIG part of balancing the spirit.

Trust who? What?

Trust your higher self.

It's the part of you that can see the big picture and always has your back.

Sometimes this means letting go of control and planning and just trusting the universe.

Some things don't need to be forced.

In the calm, you will know that all is well.

Trust will keep your spirit in a balanced state longer.

The best gift I've given myself is balance.

It's a feeling, a frequency that I carry with me wherever I go.

Try this: When you walk in nature, how long can you carry the frequency of balance after you go indoors?

Everyone's balanced spirit vibrates at a different frequency, so what feels comfortable, relaxing, and balanced to you may not feel the same to someone else.

If the frequency of meditation or music resonates with your unique frequency, it's a match, and you should continue to do it until it no longer feels good.

As your soul/spirit expands, your frequency will also expand, and you will feel a need to change your daily practices.

Try this . . .

- Do the best you can moment by moment with conscious choices to be kind, act with love, and seek the highest good of all.
- Be gentle with yourself. It's okay to put yourself first.
- Move through the day with as much heart energy or heart consciousness as possible.

- Let nature calm you.
- Go with the flow.
- Keep your heart open.
- Find a guided meditation or music that feels good to you.

A balanced spirit is pure love.

So, be in love with your home, your family, the flowers, the sky, and the strangers around you — be in love with life, and trust.

There is beauty in balance.

THE POWER OF
SPIRITUAL MATURITY

HOW TO STAY GROUNDED
IN A CHAOTIC WORLD.

WHEN YOU DESCRIBE SOMEONE AS BEING mature, do you naturally think of them as being emotionally mature?

Yes, I do too.

The thought of someone being *spiritually mature* never crossed my mind until recently.

And even in spiritual communities, where the topics of consciousness and ascension are very popular, it is rarely discussed.

Yet, it's incredibly important to the evolution of every individual.

SPIRITUAL MATURITY IS . . .

- living an authentic life that reflects your true inner self;
- great kindness to self;
- loving and caring for all living things, including Earth;
- maintaining a daily connection with higher self and universal guides;
- zero judgement of self and others;
- less ego, more heart-led actions;
- pausing before reacting;
- a curious self that is open to learn;
- sitting with discomfort when it shows up;
- striving for peace in all relationships;
- compassion first in every situation.

To me, spiritual maturity mirrors the qualities of the various dimensions that are all around us.

Each dimension holds a unique frequency, and it's common to feel a shift in ourselves when our frequency expands to match the frequency of a higher dimension.

Free will allows us to settle in a dimension for as long as we wish, until we decide to expand again to match the frequency of an even higher dimension.

Diana Cooper describes six of the spiritual dimensions in this way:

The Dimensions, by Diana Cooper

1D. The mineral kingdom operates in the first dimension. It experiences and evolves in this range. This is where new ideas root.

2D. The plant kingdom, which needs light in order to grow, evolves within the frequency of the second dimension. Here, there is an opening to spiritual information and knowledge.

3D. Those humans who only believe in a physical reality and whose hearts are closed operate within the range of the 3D frequency.

4D. People who are in the fourth dimension are beginning to open their heart chakras, remember past lives, and expand their spiritual awareness.

5D. Your heart is open. You take responsibility for all that you create and attract in your life and you do everything for the highest good of all. You wish to ascend in this lifetime and direct your energies towards that.

6D. You are living with your higher heart open. You are working with the spiritual realms, for the highest good of humanity and in cosmic service.

I can't imagine living in today's chaotic world without some daily practice that allows me to connect with myself.

Just as emotional maturity expands with practice, so does spiritual maturity.

Life gets *easier* as our spirit matures.

Because maturity creates the calm in the storm, the light in the dark, the joy in our hearts, and eventually the happiness in every moment of every day.

TO FLOW OR NOT TO FLOW

LEARNING TO LET GO OF EXPECTATIONS.

IT TOOK ME DECADES TO MANAGE MY expectations of situations and people in a confident, skillful way.

Age played an important part (age = wisdom), and exploring my spiritual self was helpful.

One day, the solution was suddenly there — like a light had been turned on — and I knew what I had to do.

Just LET GO.

Let go of expectations of how a project or a situation will flow (result: better timing of the outcome, which I had no way of knowing).

Let go of expectations of my son (result: he flourished) and a friend (result: it was time for our friendship to end, and that's okay).

LET GO OF THE OUTCOME OF SITUATIONS

Letting go of the outcome of situations took time and effort.

I practiced again and again until it happened naturally.

Whenever a situation came up that caused me to hang on too tight or insist on an outcome, I consciously pulled back.

I let go of how and when the outcome would happen.

This immediately removed all the stress and worry that occurs when you insist on a specific outcome rather than wait to see what the universe delivers in your best interest.

Being in a state of flow, versus stress and worry, gave me space to feel free.

But the best benefit was not feeling disappointed or irritated when the outcome finally revealed itself.

Here are two simple examples: When a scheduled event was moved to another date, there was no disappointment. When the plumber came in the afternoon instead of the morning as planned, I wasn't annoyed.

Every time I let go, I was pleasantly surprised and calm about the outcome, which was either what I had expected or better than I had expected.

I learned to allow the outcome of situations to flow. To expect only the best outcome. To let the universe show me what it can do. To be playful instead of tense and let the universe do its thing.

LET GO OF EXPECTATIONS OF OTHERS

Letting go of expectations of others will improve your relationships.

First, you release the burden of your expectations; second, you allow flow to exist between you and them; and third, you open up the possibility for them to surprise and delight you without the pressure of your forced expectations.

It's freedom for both parties.

Letting go does not mean that you are being passive or that you have given up.

It means your expectation has shifted — you expect only the best outcome.

When I practiced letting go of what I expected of others, it was a challenge and much more difficult than letting go of the outcome of situations.

My spiritual self had to step in and help.

I had to trust that everything would work out in a way that benefited everyone.

I leaned on my guides and angels, asking them to step in to ensure that the universe was orchestrating the best result for all (which, of course, it does whether we ask for it or not).

Sometimes I saw the goodness of the outcome right away; other times I didn't see it until months or years later, when I looked back at my life.

There were so many examples of situations with others that turned out different than how I had imagined.

And what a relief! More than a few times, the universe definitely had my back.

Just LET GO.

PHASE IV - INTERACTING WITH THE WORLD BEYOND HUMAN PERCEPTION

"The intuitive mind is a sacred gift and the rational mind is a faithful servant."
— Albert Einstein

When was the last time the universe gave you a nudge?

I often get "pushed" to say something to someone when I'm in a group or call someone who suddenly appears in my mind.

A nudge could also come in the form of an urge to watch a video or television program or read a book, where you find a message that feels like it's for you.

Even the act of blessing your food before you eat is a powerful interaction with the universe.

THE RITUAL OF CONNECTING WITH YOUR SPIRIT

SPIRITUAL TOOLS AND THE PRACTICE OF ANCIENT TRADITIONS.

THE RITUAL OF CONNECTING WITH THE human spirit has been a sacred tradition since ancient times.

When our ancestors honed their favorite practices to experience new ways to ease into deeper spiritual connections, I wonder if they knew there would be a time in history when these spiritual tools would be critical to the human race. These times are here … now.

There is a wide variety of spiritual tools available today — truly something for everybody — with meditation and sound healing the most widely known tools.

Spiritual tools guide us through challenging times, they bring us out of the fog of being stuck, and they help us remember what we've forgotten about ourselves.

When used with intention (to heal, to love oneself, to clear stuck energy, etc.), they cleanse or carry away debris from our spiritual aura, which in turn clears the channel to our higher self.

I think of these tools as my ally.

They assist me by temporarily shifting my vibration to a higher level.

And when one tool doesn't resonate with me, I try another one — a spiritual match always reveals itself.

HERE'S A SHORT LIST OF SOME OF THE MOST COMMON SPIRITUAL TOOLS

- spiritual books, videos, conferences, online events
- group ceremonies, e.g., cacao ceremony, spring equinox
- earthing, e.g., walking barefoot on the Earth
- Reiki, energy healing
- meditation
- intuition
- breathwork
- crystals
- sound healing
- sacred geometry
- affirmations
- mantras
- forest bathing
- oracle cards

- numerology
- tuning forks
- smudging
- music
- essential oils

TRY A TOOL THAT'S NEW TO YOU

It's fun to try something new!

If you saw one or two tools on the list that piqued your interest, do a little research on the topic.

Let's say you want to know more about forest bathing. What is it? Is it available near you? Do an online search with your location to find these answers.

I searched and found blog posts, events, retreats, and tips about forest bathing.

Perhaps you are interested in crystals. Do an online search to find metaphysical stores in your area. The folks who work at these stores have a wealth of knowledge about spiritual tools, including crystals.

I've also attended gemstone events in my town, where I met people who are passionate about crystals and gemstones.

If you research or try a tool and discover it doesn't resonate with you, move on to another tool.

Don't settle for something that's not supporting your spiritual growth.

You might also experience fatigue with a particular spiritual tool.

If you have been attending a meditation group for over a year and you're no longer excited about attending, try another group. You'll meet new people and possibly learn a new meditation method.

Also, as your spirit grows and expands, it will want to explore new tools.

There are many options on purpose; use what resonates with your spirit at any given time.

CONNECT WITH YOUR SPIRIT AT ANY AGE

Some people think exploring the spiritual self happens at a certain age: *I'll try meditation when I'm 50.*

This isn't true at all.

When you were born, your spirit had already had eons of experience expanding and growing.

This lifetime on Earth is simply another opportunity to expand and grow in a new set of circumstances.

You are a spiritual being having a human experience.

The spiritual journey only continues; it never ends.

WHAT WISDOM WILL THE ORACLE CARDS SHARE TODAY?

MEDITATING WITH MY SPIRIT GUIDE.

Note: Oracle cards should not be confused with tarot cards. Tarot is a method of divination, while oracle cards simply offer guidance, affirmations, and emotional support.

WHEN I'M MENTALLY OR EMOTIONALLY working through something, it's not always comfortable to lean on a friend.

Then I remember I have a team of guides, angels, and transitioned loved ones who are just waiting to offer a bit of guidance.

One of my favorite ways to communicate with them is through oracle cards.

It starts with a question. Usually, I ask, *What do I need to know right now?*

The question is infused with focus and intention while I shuffle the cards.

This continues until I *feel* the answer.

That's the moment I reveal the top card and begin to interpret the guidance from my spirit guide.

WORDS AND IMAGES are deeply powerful, which is why oracle cards are an excellent spiritual tool.

And because they are designed to uplift, inspire, and offer guidance, they're available in almost any topic that inspires you.

Here are just a few …

lightworker, Gaia, goddesses, Reiki, I Ching, crystals, shaman, witches and wizards, Kuan Yin, wild Australia, totem, angels, Buddhism, astrology, Hawaii, medicine, ascension, magick, Norse, animals, dragons, herbs, unicorns, Celtic, Lemuria, chakras, Goddess Isis, fairies, druids, Day of the Dead, mermaids, Mother Mary, alchemist, Rumi, inner child, dreams, ancestors, trees

---

I HAVE A ZILLION INTERESTS, so I have multiple decks around the house.

This works well for me because when I feel inspired to ask a question, I prefer to select a deck that matches my mood.

HERE ARE THE STEPS THAT WORK FOR ME WHEN SELECTING AND USING AN ORACLE CARD DECK

Select a deck. The topic pulls me in at first, but I also consider the words of wisdom on the cards and the illustrations (imagining how they will be part of my meditations). Each deck is infused with a story and energy from the author and the illustrator, so I look for one that speaks to me energetically. I take my time with this task. I listen intuitively to know which deck resonates with my energy field.

Clear the cards before using them. I always clear the energy of the cards before using them. This is a good practice for all spiritual tools, including crystals, jewelry, and so on. I light an incense stick or sage bundle and let the smoke infuse the cards for about a minute while I imagine any negative residue drifting away in the smoke.

Get to know the cards. Once I have selected a deck, I sit awhile with the cards, studying the illustrations and reading the words of wisdom. I send love to the cards. I ask them to help me connect with my inner wisdom and guide me.

Light a candle. This helps bring me into the moment and lets my guides know I'm ready to connect with them.

Breathe. I close my eyes and take a deep breath in for the count of 3 seconds, hold it for 6 seconds, and exhale for 9 seconds. As I breathe, I ask my spirit guides to join me.

Shuffle the cards. I think about my question: *What do I need to know right now? What guidance do I need today?* My full attention is on the question while I shuffle the cards. This continues until I *feel* the answer.

Reveal the guidance. When I feel the answer to my question, I cut the deck in half and flip the top card to reveal my guide's guidance.

Interpret the guidance. I spend a few minutes with the card, considering my immediate impressions. What do the words mean to me? How does the illustration support the words? Then I read the card's description in the booklet that's included with the cards.

Thank my spirit guide for the guidance. When I'm done, I close the meditation session by thanking my spirit guide. If I feel prompted, I write a few words in my meditation notebook.

Observe the card periodically throughout the day. There are days when it's nice to be reminded of my guide's message throughout the day. To do this, I either put the card on my desk or take a photo of it so it's with me wherever I go.

Do you have a favorite oracle deck that you use to connect with your guides, angels, and transitioned loved ones? Drop me a note and let me know.

USING A PENDULUM
TO READ ENERGY

PRACTICAL AND INTUITIVE APPLICATIONS.

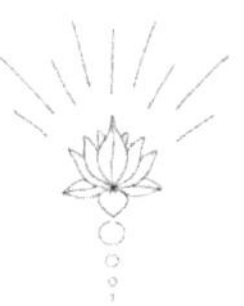

AN INTEREST IN EVERYTHING RELATED TO energy healing, including methods and tools, prompted me to purchase a pear-shaped beechwood pendulum from the Metaphysical Research Group.

Mostly, it's an excellent energy tool that assists me (as a practitioner) before and during a Reiki session when I need a deeper understanding of the health of a client's front and back chakras.

My hands can detect energy from the chakras, but the pendulum boosts the energy and then communicates with me by swinging in a particular direction when it's held over a chakra. I use a list of 17 different tested motions or swings to get a deeper understanding of each chakra's current state.

The way it works is the energy in my hand travels down the chain, surrounds the pendulum's energy field, interacts with the client's chakra, and then swings in a particular way depending on the level of energy detected.

TESTING FOOD AND SUPPLEMENTS

Because of a pendulum's ability to magnify energy levels, I also use it to test the effectiveness of herbal supplements.

I place my left hand on the supplement bottle, hold the pendulum with my right hand, and then I ask if the product is good for my body.

The pendulum swings in a vertical direction for yes and a horizontal direction for no (your yes/no swings may be different than mine).

This method is also helpful when you want to test food, drinks, or anything consumed, especially if you suspect a food allergy.

IT'S A TEMPORARY TOOL

Over time, you will get used to the pendulum and how it communicates.

Even if it remains still after you ask a question, it is communicating with you.

When there is no swing, it usually means *neutral* or *ask again at another time*.

Eventually, there will be a moment when you sense that you no longer need the tool, because when you focus on a yes/no question, you instantly hear the answer.

Two additional methods

Muscle testing (kinesiology) is used by chiropractors and energy practitioners to access yes/no feedback from a client.

I've also noticed a new trend in the spiritual community — the use of L-shaped dowsing rods to gather guidance by asking yes/no questions.

Resources

- Metaphysical Research Group, https://www.metaphysicalresearchgroup.co.uk/
- Dowsing Charts, https://www.subtil.net/en/
- The American Society of Dowsers, https://americansocietyofdowser-s.wildapricot.org/

ARE SPIRITUAL TOOLS GIVING AWAY YOUR POWER?

HOW TO USE TOOLS WITHOUT LOSING YOUR INTUITION.

I KNOW IT'S A HUMAN THING, BUT IT STILL amazes me how much energy we put into wanting to know what's going to happen next.

Does it really matter? Whatever we think it is, it could change in an instant.

Perhaps "knowing" the future makes us feel better for a moment or temporarily calms our anxiety.

We make appointments with psychics. We spread a few tarot cards. We consult a pendulum or an astrology chart.

And after a while, all of this desire to "know" begins to feel . . . exhausting.

I'm definitely guilty of turning to these future-seeking methods (and also highly recommend them), but if they are not consumed in moderation, knowledge seeking can easily become an addiction.

When I noticed the addictive behavior in myself, I purposely pulled back and started to practice checking in with myself if I needed to know something instead of looking outside myself for guidance. I wanted to reclaim my power and not give it away to tarot cards, channelers, and spiritual teachers.

You create your future

If taken too far, spiritual tools become an excuse to disconnect from personal responsibility.

For example, fear and insecurity can drive an obsessive need to read tarot or listen to spiritual teachers.

What's going to happen?

What do I need to do?

A healthier option would be to trust, breathe, calm yourself, and visualize the future you intuitively know you want.

If you can manage the panic with a few minutes of calm, the fear will go away, and you will hear what you need to know.

Eventually, you won't want to use a tool (tarot, pendulum, psychic) to feel connected to your inner wisdom.

You'll realize that you were born with the ability to intuitively hear, feel, or sense your higher self.

While it's nice once in a while to get validation, the information from these spiritual tools is simply a reflection of what you instinctually already know.

It's time to honor your innate sacred gifts.

PHASE V - HEALING, LOSS AND TRANSFORMATION

"What is loved is never lost."
— Helen Keller

Healing requires a willingness to transform without expectations. Trust is key.

Whatever is needed, the healing method, and the outcome, will always show up in a way that's in your best interest.

Even the deepest wound — when someone leaves this world — will be healed with love and a deep awakening.

MY FIRST ENERGY
HEALING EXPERIENCE

ONE DAY, I WAS IN A PARTICULARLY CURIOUS mood. I wondered what circumstances had to occur in my life for a pivotal moment to fall into place.

I wrote down the names of people who (unknowingly) played a part in the pivotal moment. Then I noted the events that were connected to the moment.

Once I had the details in front of me, it was clear there was a pattern.

Had there been one slight change, the pivotal moment may not have happened.

Plus, when I was experiencing each key event, they appeared to be ordinary and unconnected.

But years later, when I looked at the whole picture, nothing was random. One event led to another event and then another in an orderly sequence to gently push me in a direction that was meant for me, but I could never have imagined.

____

"If you want to find the secrets of the universe, think in terms of energy, frequency, and vibration."
— Nikola Tesla

____

IT STARTED Christmas 2003 when a dear friend gave me a gift certificate for a Swedish massage.

It was one of her favorite indulgences, and she wanted me to experience something that she enjoyed (it wasn't a privilege I had done in the past or would have purchased myself).

A few months later, I booked an appointment and was welcomed by Anthony (the salon's only massage therapist).

We got started, and after an hour had passed, I was very relaxed and enjoying the experience.

During the last few minutes of the session, I was lying face down on the massage table when I felt something non-physical move across my back.

Whatever it was, it had mass but not physical mass.

From my position, I couldn't see Anthony's hands, but I could feel them about a foot above my body; he was pulling at something in the space between my body and his hands.

More than once, he moved the mass away from me and dropped it on the floor.

It was unusual and remarkable all at once.

When the session was over, he kindly walked me to my car. I was glad. I had questions.

Yes, I wanted to know what he had done at the end of the session (the technique), but that was secondary.

What I really wanted to know . . . why was I feeling the way I was feeling?

It was a state of being that I had never experienced. My whole self (emotional, spiritual, mental, and physical) felt light, floating, unburdened, extremely calm, and incredible.

I was in such a euphoric state that I was having trouble speaking.

When I asked what technique he used at the end of the session, when he moved something off my back, he casually replied, "Oh, I was trained in Reiki in Central California. Whenever I give a massage, if I sense the client is open to energy healing, I go ahead and do that too."

What?! I thought. *What's energy healing? What's Reiki?*

I carried that euphoric feeling around with me for almost three weeks.

The experience was so loving and healing, so otherworldly, that I spent more than a decade trying to duplicate the feeling (without success).

I now know that every experience has its own purpose and timing and can't be duplicated, only expanded.

The purpose of that experience in 2004 was to shine a light on energy healing and the non-physical energy all around us.

It was one of my life's pivotal moments that today continues to shape me and the way I see the world and the universe.

HEALING AFTER SOMEONE YOU LOVE TRANSITIONS

YOU CAN MAINTAIN A CONNECTION BEYOND THE PHYSICAL.

THE PASSING OF SOMEONE CLOSE TO YOU IS A sensitive subject.

It's extremely personal.

It's unique to everybody.

And it's one of those transformative human experiences that cannot be avoided and is completely out of your control.

The only next step is through it, and no two people grieve and heal in the same way for someone (e.g., a mother heals differently than a father when a child passes).

It's a heavy, heavy lesson to carry throughout life, but there are ways to heal.

What hurts the most is the loss of their physical presence.

You are left to live your life without their physical self.

But this doesn't mean you can't commune with their spirit or non-physical self. You can.

It's a very real option if you allow it.

It requires an expansion of your spiritual self in ways that may seem unconventional in our conditioned world, but who cares?

Our souls have incarnated into this lifetime to expand, to learn, and to experience human life.

Feel free during your healing process to do whatever heals your soul, regardless of what others may think.

There are endless ways to heal, but I relied on three approaches over many years to navigate the loss of a spouse, a brother, a pet, and friends.

HELP FROM A MEDIUM

Sitting with a medium who is able to connect with your loved one is life-changing and unforgettable.

And depending on your healing process and your experience, it may be one of the most healing steps you take.

The only challenge is finding a medium who is able to connect with your loved one. Sometimes there's no connection. Your loved one may not be ready to connect. Or other family members or friends who have passed may dominate the session. It's not up to the medium to decide who comes through during a session. You may have to visit two or three mediums over a period of time.

You can also help by thinking about or talking to your loved one before a session; ask them to be with you during the session.

When the medium connects with your loved one, you will feel it. It will feel as if he or she is standing in the room with you.

Your body may tingle, the hairs on your arms may stand upright, or you may get goosebumps. That's their energy connecting with your energy. Be open to whatever comes through.

BE OPEN TO A VISIT FROM YOUR LOVED ONE'S SPIRIT

When my husband passed, he visited me in a dream about a month after his transition. His passing was unexpected and immediate, so I'm sure it took him a few weeks to adjust.

I later had a knowing that he wanted to communicate with me as soon as he could, because his passing had been so sudden. The easiest way for a spirit to connect with us is in a dream state, which is why he chose this communication method.

I have never had a loved one visit me in a dream; he

was the only one. It's also the only dream I've been able to remember; it was that real and vivid.

He showed up wearing his favorite faux leather jacket (this made me chuckle). He didn't say a word the entire time we were together. We either communicated with a glance or telepathically.

Mostly we just stood together on the grass by the lake, as if he was reading my state of being in our closeness. I expressed that I would be okay, and there was no need for him to worry or visit me anymore.

Years later, when my brother transitioned, I was grateful he was there to greet him; they were good friends.

I've never felt disconnected from his spirit.

We're connected differently, but we're still connected.

That's what matters, and it gives me great comfort to know that he's standing on the sidelines, offering his support when I ask for it.

A LOVED ONE may not come in a dream.

Most of the time, they will nudge you to get your attention.

You'll experience a rush feeling in your upper body, and an image of your loved one will flash in your mind's eye.

That's when you'll know the nudge was from their spirit.

MY BROTHER GAVE me two clear nudges within the first 18 months of his transition.

When he was born, he was "blessed" with red/orange hair. While this color was common where I grew up, it was very unusual where I lived when he passed.

On the anniversary of his passing, I was thinking of him as I drove past the local high school, which I did most days.

There, walking on the sidewalk in front of the school, was a tall girl with red/orange hair!

I couldn't believe it.

I had driven past the school hundreds of times and never saw anyone with this color hair. But on the anniversary, when I was thinking of him, there she was in plain sight.

I've never seen her since, and I still drive past the school often.

It was as if she was there just for that one moment; his way of saying hello.

The second time he nudged me was the day I received the keys to a house I decided to purchase after his passing.

I visited him a few months before he transitioned, and while I was there, he asked me if I liked dragonflies. I wasn't sure where that was coming from until he said he had noticed the tiny dragonfly earrings I was wearing.

Shortly after he transitioned, I started looking for a home to buy.

During the long process, I often talked to him and asked for his help and real estate expertise because he had been a real estate agent.

On the day I finally received the keys, I took a few minutes to walk through the house on my own.

I was in a high-vibrational state, with an overall feeling of gratitude.

I went upstairs and looked out the bedroom window at the beautiful courtyard. That's when I noticed a dragonfly flying high in the sky next to the tree near the window. Seconds later, the dragonfly flew in front of the window where I was standing (about eight inches away); it positioned itself at eye level with me, held itself in mid-air, and locked eyes with me for a moment.

I wasn't thinking about my brother at the time, but I knew instantly that the dragonfly was his spirit. He was there to say congratulations.

I RECEIVED another gentle nudge from my maternal grandfather. He was special and very intuitive.

When I was growing up, he often pulled me aside to secretly slip a silver dollar into my hand, to my sheer delight. This happened every time he drove to our house from out of state with my grandmother.

When he transitioned, I was in Puerto Rico with my cell phone turned off.

The day I was to return home, everyone in the group was asked to pack their things, clean out their sleeping tent, and wait on the patio for a ride to the airport.

When I finished my tasks, I turned on my phone and saw a message from my brother; our grandfather had died a few days ago at his home.

I returned to the patio, feeling a bit sad. I shared with a few people in the group that he had transitioned and had lived a happy life with my grandmother; he was 100 years old.

We were then asked by our host to bring our pillows to the main house (we were previously asked to leave them in our tent).

I walked to the tent where I had slept and bent down to unzip the zipper to get inside.

That's when I noticed it. Halfway up the zipper (on the zipper, where it couldn't fall or be missed) was a shiny penny!

I was so shocked I stepped back from the tent, not believing what I was seeing.

Where did the coin come from? Everyone in the group was on the patio. When I closed up the tent, I zipped it myself.

There was no other explanation.

It was one last coin from my sweet grandfather.

EVERY TIME I GET A NUDGE, I'm in a calm state, sometimes thinking about the person, sometimes not.

Connecting with them doesn't take any effort on my part.

My job is to pay attention.

I've also noticed that their assistance is elevated beyond what they were able to do when they were in a human body. This is the universe in play.

I have fun with it, I enjoy it, and I'm truly grateful for the support.

TALK ABOUT YOUR LOVED ONE

Your life story includes people who have transitioned; therefore, your happy memories with them belong in your conversations.

The people in your life want to hear these stories because they help them understand what life events have shaped you.

It's not necessary to talk about the sad and painful memories that pull you and everyone else down. Share the joyful experiences or moments that elevate your energy.

Two magical things happen when you talk about your loved one.

First, you keep the happy moments of their life alive and in the hearts of the people around you.

Second, the joy you feel when you share happy memories raises the vibration of your energy (you may feel it in the heart area).

This is important because your loved one's spirit exists at a higher plane, one that vibrates higher than Earth's plane.

When you share a happy memory and are vibrating higher, your loved one can pick up the vibe.

There will be a brief moment when you will feel their essence in the room.

Don't be afraid to share your memories when you feel the need; your loved one enjoys visiting and feeling the love in the room.

IN CLOSING

I didn't grieve and heal the same for every loved one who passed.

Many factors influenced how I felt, including my age, the role the person played in my life, how quickly or slowly the person transitioned, whether or not I was able to say goodbye, and my experience with grief and loss.

However, there was one common thread across all of them: my knowing that they are never really gone.

I still feel their essence in random ways.

PHASE VI - EXPANSION BEYOND THE SELF

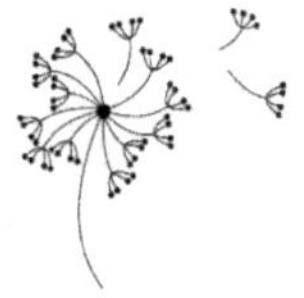

"You are not a drop in the ocean. You are the entire ocean in a drop."
— Rumi

The universe is massive, beyond anything we could ever imagine.

For eons, it's been full of creators (like you and me), simple and complex worlds, conflict between species, and a whole lot more — all for the purpose of experiencing something new, expanding deeper, and learning from the yin and yang.

Part of our life journey is to explore the universe, not to hold onto ideas as the only truth, but to dig deeper, change our minds along the way, and give each other grace to follow a path that's our own.

TRAVEL: THE ULTIMATE SPIRITUAL TEACHER

EXPERIENCES THAT ENCOURAGE YOU TO TURN UP YOUR INTUITION.

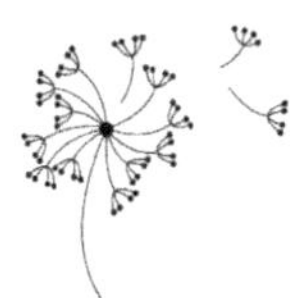

In 2001, I backpacked Western Europe with my 17-year-old son, who had just graduated from high school.

Our itinerary highlighted things to see and do in six countries during the month of June.

When we arrived back in California in early July, I was a different person.

My physical and emotional self was the same, but my spiritual self was wide awake and processing the experiences of the trip.

This was a nice surprise, but I didn't know what to do with it.

My spiritual self wasn't something I had been developing at that time in my life.

It's common to hear people say, *I love to travel.*

They love it because it's new, interesting, and a change of pace. But what they don't think about is what it does to their inner self.

Travel offers fresh experiences in a new environment while it deepens your understanding of people.

In a foreign land, you may be unable to read or speak the language, the food may not be familiar, and the culture and customs may require interpretation and an adjustment in the way you act in the world.

Here are more ways your spiritual self is tested:

- Your inner guidance and intuition become more heightened;
- You must trust strangers to help you or give you information;
- Your connection to nature may expand if you visit a forest, mountain, or ocean;
- Your view of the world changes because of all your new experiences;
- Your beliefs get tested;
- Your role in the world resurfaces and becomes part of your consciousness.

These new experiences test your spiritual self because they create a feeling of being off balance.

To regain balance, an adjustment of self and an opening of the heart often need to occur.

***

WHEN MY SON and I first arrived in Western Europe, everything was different — the food, sounds, cars, driving rules, transportation options, and the language — but I was more than happy to embrace it all.

Then we arrived in Italy, and everything shifted.

Italy was determined to test me, and it did.

To stay on schedule, we opted to ride an overnight train to Rome, arriving in the morning so we had the afternoon to visit the coliseum. When we arrived, I was exhausted. Sleeping on the train had been impossible. I was glad we had reservations at a nearby pensione; I needed a two-hour nap before lunch and exploring the city. The innkeeper didn't speak English, and I didn't speak Italian, but I managed to communicate that I was exhausted and needed to rest. I showed her a copy of our reservation and asked if we could check in an hour early if our room was available. Her mood immediately went from polite to angry. She shooed us out the door and told us to come back in an hour. I wanted to push the topic a bit to get the key, but my senses told me to let it go; if I gave her any lip, she'd pull our reservation and we wouldn't have a place to stay. It seemed ridiculous that we had to walk down the street and hang out for an hour when our room was ready to occupy. An hour later she showed us to our very simple room, and that was the end of the drama.

When it was time to leave the pensione and travel to our next city, I approached her with my Italian phrasebook open (no convenient phone translation apps in 2001) and a serious look on my face. I wanted her to know that I was determined to communicate with her in her language, since it was such a big deal when I checked in. She tried to say something, but I put my hand up to stop her, to ask her to wait. She smiled and looked pleased as I did my best to say what I needed to say. It was clear from her body language and kind manner that I had done the right thing. All she wanted was for me to make an effort to speak her language. To her, it was a symbol of respect.

And then there was the day before we left Rome and the man in the ticket booth at the Sistine Chapel who didn't like the look on my son's face. Before I knew what was happening, the man was yelling something at us in Italian (and making a huge scene). When my son ignored him (typical teenager), he really got angry and came out of the booth to yell in his face. Somehow, I was able to defuse the situation, and he sold us (reluctantly) two tickets. All these years later, I still have no idea why he acted in such an extreme manner.

A few days later, in Siena, Italy, it was late in the day when we got on the city bus at the train station. I realized we missed our stop when the bus started traveling out of the city and into the country, where there were a few homes. We were the last passengers on the bus. I tried to communicate with the driver (in broken Italian and my phrasebook) that we had missed our stop. He looked very angry and didn't want to hear what I had to say, so I returned to my seat. When he got to the last stop on his route, he thundered over to us and screamed something in Italian. The only word I understood was finito (finished), which included wild arm gestures toward the door. We exited the bus, and he drove away, leaving us stranded in a strange country in the middle of nowhere just as the sun was setting and the sky was getting dark. I turned to look behind me and saw an older Italian couple standing in front of their country home, looking at us, just as shocked as we were. The only option we had was to follow the road the bus had taken, assuming it would lead us back into town.

OVER THE YEARS, travel has been my favorite spiritual teacher.

The experiences and situations I find myself in expand my thinking, force me to look at the world from others' perspectives, and show me that people everywhere want the same thing.

My job is to show up with an open heart, a kind spirit,

and my intuition turned way up; that's when everything falls into place, in my best interest.

HOW DOLORES CANNON EXPANDED SPIRITUAL AWARENESS

WE LIVE IN AN ABUNDANT UNIVERSE WHERE ANYTHING IS POSSIBLE.

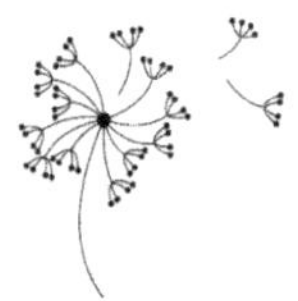

IN 2019, WHEN I HAD AN URGE TO EXPLORE NEW spiritual content, I followed a friend's recommendation and picked up a book by Dolores Cannon. One book led me to another, and another, and another until I had consumed five of her books.

- The Convoluted Universe (Book 2)
- The Convoluted Universe (Book 3)
- The Convoluted Universe (Book 4)
- The Convoluted Universe (Book 5)
- The Three Waves of Volunteers and the New Earth

Without a doubt, Cannon's books helped me open a whole new way of observing my spiritual self, my life here on Earth, and the universe.

"Everything known and unknown is hidden in the recesses of the subconscious where it awaits discovery."
— Dolores Cannon

IF YOU'RE NOT familiar with her work, she developed a safe and effective hypnosis method referred to as Quantum Healing Hypnosis Technique (QHHT).

Using this method, she was able to help clients talk to their subconscious (higher self), allowing them to understand how to heal their body, untangle karma, explore past lives, and countless other topics.

The information revealed by her clients' subconscious (higher self) is truly mind-blowing (then you realize it's information we all knew before we were born, but quickly forgot).

In her books, Cannon reveals content that sounds out of this world (because it is). Don't let this scare you off. Just sit with the truth and an open mind. Let the content simmer awhile.

Read her books with discernment and a deep curiosity to know the truth that's been hidden for thousands of years.

A FEW LESSONS I LEARNED FROM CANNON'S BOOKS

Anything is possible. Our essence or spirit wants to continuously learn and expand, so it has chosen to experience all types of lives, including etheric higher-dimensional lives, physical lives on other planets, and plant, animal, and mineral lives.

We are galactic beings. There is so much more to us than this human life we're living. This knowledge led me to research the history of our galaxy and the beings who were part of the evolution. I also worked with John Napolitano (Nap) to tap into my own personal galactic Akashic records.

We are eternal, multidimensional beings living all our lives at the same time — past, present, and future. Linear time does not exist beyond Earth. When we sleep, our dreams show us a glimpse of some of these lives.

The purpose of all human life is to learn self-love and to expand our spirit to a higher level of consciousness. To love others, you must first love yourself. It is a gift to live a human life that offers an opportunity to expand your spirit.

WE LIVE in a time when information about our world and universe is spilling out of every crevice, just waiting for us to discover what's been hidden and to help us remember what we've forgotten.

In a big way, Cannon's books have an important mission during this time — to elevate the spiritual thought of thousands of people.

I know there is something for everyone in her books, whether you're looking to understand aspects of this lifetime or discover more about yourself.

Start with one of her books and see where it leads you. Happy reading!

THE SPIRITUAL BOOKS
THAT SHAPED MY JOURNEY

WISDOM FROM TEACHERS YOU
MAY — OR MAY NOT — KNOW.

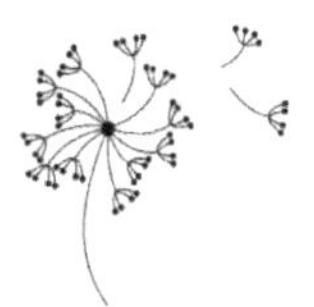

ONCE PEOPLE KNOW I HAVE AN INTEREST IN spiritual metaphysical topics, they often ask what books I've read. So, I compiled a list of the books in my home library.

I grouped them into five categories:

ENERGY HEALING

SPIRITUAL GROWTH

REINCARNATION/NEAR-DEATH EXPERIENCE

CHANNELED WISDOM

HEALTH & WELLNESS.

I hope somewhere in this list you find a book or two that you feel inclined to explore.

ENERGY HEALING

I've been interested in energy healing since my Reiki training in 2020 and 2021. Energy healing is based on the fact that everything has a frequency and an energy pattern, including the human body. Energy work has been used for thousands of years to balance the body's energy fields and, if an illness is present, to guide divine energy so that it helps the body heal itself.

Exploring Vibrational Medicine, Richard Gerber, M.D.

Energy Work: The Secrets of Healing and Spiritual Growth, Robert Bruce

Energy Work: The Secret of Healing and Spiritual Development, Robert Bruce

The Healing Power of Reiki, Raven Keyes

Medical Reiki: A Groundbreaking Approach to Using Energy Medicine for Challenging Treatments, Raven Keyes

The Emotion Code, Dr. Bradley Nelson

The Body Code, Dr. Bradley Nelson

Hands of Light: A Guide to Healing Through the Human Energy Field, Barbara Ann Brennan

Hands That Heal, Echo Bodine

Energy Medicine: Balancing Your Body's Energies

for Optimal Health, Joy and Vitality, Donna Eden with David Feinstein, Ph.D.

Universal Truths: Unlocking the Secrets to Energy Healing, Wayne & Wanda Cook

Energy Medicine: Use Your Body's Energies, Donna Eden

Tuning the Human Biofield: Healing with Vibrational Sound Therapy, Eileen Day McKusick

Chakra Healing, Margarita Alcantara

5 Elements of Sound Healing, Bodhi Starwater

Angelic Reiki, Christine Core

SPIRITUAL GROWTH

I often talk to people who are thinking about their spiritual growth. If they want to start slow, I suggest *Travels* by Michael Crichton or *The Alchemist*. If they want to dive in deep, David Hawkins' book *Letting Go* is a good place to begin. There's no best place to start, but to narrow it down, I always advise them to use their instincts — select something that stands out.

Letting Go: The Pathway to Surrender, David R. Hawkins

Going Within: A Guide for Inner Transformation, Shirley MacLaine

When God Winks: How the Power of Coincidence Guides Your Life, Squire Rushnell

Developing Intuition: Practical Guidance for Daily Life, Shakti Gawain

A New Earth: Awakening to Your Life's Purpose, Eckhart Tolle

The Power of Now: A Guide to Spiritual Enlightenment, Eckhart Tolle

Travels, Michael Crichton

The Alchemist, Paulo Coelho

The Seat of the Soul, Gary Zukav

Chicken Soup for the Soul: Angels Among Us, 101 Inspirational Stories, Jack Canfield, Mark Victor Hansen, Amy Newmark

The Four Agreements, Don Miguel Ruiz

The Wisdom of the Shamans, Don Jose Ruiz

Love Beyond Words: 356 Days of Inspiration from Spirit, Suzanne Giesemann

The Book of Secrets: Unlocking the Hidden Dimensions of Your Life, Deepak Chopra

Kitchen Table Wisdom, Rachel Naomi Remen

Sabbath: Restoring the Sacred Rhythm of Rest, Wayne Muller

The Dance, Oriah Mountain Dreamer

The Automatic Writing Experience (AWE): How to Turn Your Journaling into Channeling to Get Unstuck, Find Direction, and Live Your Greatest Life, Michael Sandler

Waking Up in Time: Finding Inner Peace in Times of Accelerating Change, Peter Russell

The Archangel Guide to Ascension: 55 Steps to the Light, Diana Cooper & Tim Whild

The Law of One: Book 1, The Ra Material, Elkins, Rueckert, McCarty

Wherever You Go There You Are: Mindfulness Meditation in Everyday Life, Jon Kabat-Zinn

How to Read the Akashic Records, Linda Howe

A Radical Approach to the Akashic Records, Master Your Life and Raise Your Vibration, Melissa Feick

Enchanted Love: The Mystical Power of Intimate Relationships, Marianne Williamson

The Aladdin Factor, Jack Canfield & Mark Victor Hansen

In Search of Grace, Kristin Hahn

REINCARNATION/NEAR-DEATH EXPERIENCE

My interest in near-death experiences and reincarnation started decades ago when I began exploring all things metaphysical. I had lots of questions: *Where do we go when we die? Why do we live multiple lives? Why are certain people in our lives?* Years later, I learned we have lives between lives — something I had not thought of.

Many Lives, Many Masters, Brian L. Weiss, M.D.

Miracles Happen: The Transformational Healing Power of Past-Life Memories, Brian L. Weiss, M.D. & Amy E. Weiss

Messages from the Masters: Tapping into the Power of Love, Brian L. Weiss

Life Between Life: Scientific Exploration into the Void Separating One Incarnation from the Next, Joel L. Whitton, M.D., Ph.D.

Embraced by the Light, Betty J. Eadie

A Call From the Other Side, Sue Nicholson

Channeled Wisdom

The popularity of channeling has grown in the past decade. Ruth Montgomery, Dolores Cannon, and Paul Selig are my current favorites.

Threshold to Tomorrow, Ruth Montgomery

Here and Hereafter, Ruth Montgomery

Companions Along the Way, Ruth Montgomery

The Convoluted Universe (Book 4), Dolores Cannon

The Convoluted Universe (Book 5), Dolores Cannon

Five Lives Remembered, Dolores Cannon

Between Death and Life: Conversations with a Spirit, Dolores Cannon

The Search for Hidden, Sacred Knowledge, Dolores Cannon

Keepers of the Garden, Dolores Cannon

The Three Waves of Volunteers and the New Earth, Dolores Cannon

The Soul Truth: A guide to Inner Peace, Sheila and Marcus Gillette and the teachings of THEO

The Book of Love and Creation: A Channeled Text, Paul Selig

Ask and it is Given: Learning to Manifest Your Desires, Esther & Jerry Hicks

Manifestation Mastery: How to Shift Your Reality & Co-Create with the Universe, Christina Rice

Conversations with Spirit: The Truth About Death and Reincarnation, Robert H. Skye

2012 and Beyond: An Invitation to Meet the Challenges and Opportunities Ahead, Diana Cooper

The Golden Future, Diana Cooper

The Top 10 Things Dead People Want to Tell YOU, Mike Dooley

You Can't Make This Stuff Up, Theresa Caputo

Angels in my Hair, Lorna Byrne

Evidence of Eternity, Mark Anthony

HEALTH & WELLNESS

It wasn't until I was older that I understood how in sync the sacred triangle, body-mind-spirit, must be for optimal health. A body that is not well cared for will pull the whole triangle down. While a body that is healthy and cared for day after day lifts the three elements higher than you can imagine.

The Jungle Search for Nature's Cures, Nicole Maxwell

The Seven Circles: Indigenous Teachings for Living Well, Chelsey Luger & Thosh Collins

Medical Medium: Secrets Behind Chronic and Mystery Illness and How to Finally Heal, Anthony William

Why People Don't Heal and How They Can, Caroline Myss, Ph.D.

Anatomy of the Spirit: The Seven Stages of Power and Healing, Caroline Myss, Ph.D.

The Energy Codes: The 7-Step System to Awaken Your Spirit, Heal Your Body, and Live Your Best Life, Sue Morter

The Body Electric, Robert O. Becker, M.D. & Gary Selden

The Hidden Messages in Water, Masaru Emoto

Messages from Water and the Universe, Masaru Emoto

Mudras: Yoga in your Hands, Gertrud Hirschi

WHAT'S your favorite spiritual book? I'd love to know what inspires you. Drop me a note and let me know.

Happy reading.

"What we give away is what we keep."
— Unknown

It's the mature generations who can remind the young generations that life is a journey.

And the most important lesson that you appreciate along the way is . . . life is a GIFT.

You feel. You learn. You love. You remember who you are.

A LETTER TO MY GRANDDAUGHTER

STEP FORWARD INTO THE FUTURE WITH CURIOSITY AND EXCITEMENT.

MY DEAR, SWEET TALULA—

Today, as you celebrate your 18th birthday, I thank the universe for blessing me and the world with your presence. You have always been a kind, loving spirit that everyone who knows you wants to be around. This makes me very proud.

The adventure in front of you is exciting. You have chosen a lifetime that will be unlike any other time in Earth's history. Trust this knowledge. Let your imagination go wild. Design the life you desire. History has no claim on your future.

As you move forward, I ask that you take the tidbits of wisdom below with you.

Tap into your inner self on a regular basis. Commune with your spirit as well as your helpers, guides, ancestors, and galactic family who are always close to you, just in a different frequency.

Be true to your path. Only do what brings you joy. And always follow your entrepreneurial spirit.

Be grateful every day. Do little things for others often. Both acts of kindness will feed your soul.

Don't hold back your truth. Anything can be said in a kind way, even your truth.

Spend time alone. Get to know yourself. Recharge your energy. Love yourself, always.

Surround yourself with people who are kind, grateful, hardworking, and honest. This will naturally happen when you are the person you want to attract.

Don't waste your time on toxic relationships; end them quickly. This is important and includes all relationships, even family members.

Balance is critical. This includes all areas of your life: friends, family, food, activity, work, and self-care. Find what helps you rebalance these areas on a regular basis.

Nurture and expand your creative gifts. To be inspired, surround yourself with music, art, reading, photography — all the arts. Embrace your imagination. It's your power source.

Move your body every day. Your body likes to move; it was designed to move. It will help you maintain a balanced mind, body, and spirit. Dance until you're 108.

Your health is critical to achieving your mission during this lifetime. Be your own doctor. No one knows your body better than you; learn to know what it needs by using your intuition.

Rest your mind and body. Get 7–8 hours of sleep every night.

Keep traveling. Your spirit loves to travel. Visit a new place every year. Meet new people. Eat their food. Understand all peoples of the world.

Your adult years are a training environment for your soul. It's a time when you will experience most of your life lessons. You will also discover, *Why am I here? What do I need to learn in this lifetime?*

T, step forward into the future with curiosity and excitement. Let everything else fall away. You got this!

All my love,

Nonna

August 2025

DEDICATION

This book is dedicated to the archangels, guides, and loved ones in the light who have stood with me in this lifetime. I am truly grateful.

Hello, dear reader. I need your help. If you enjoyed I'M NO LONGER THE WEIRD ONE IN THE ROOM, I'd love your feedback. Please consider leaving a review on Amazon and Goodreads. All authors depend on reviews to get the word out about their books. Thank you.

Goodreads

ABOUT THE AUTHOR

Shine Redwood is an author and Reiki master who has been interested in spiritual metaphysics since an early age.

She enjoys connecting with people who are curious about their spiritual self and are open to exploring topics such as energy healing, galactic history, divination, telepathy, spirit guides, intuition, reincarnation, tarot, dowsing, communicating with those who have left Earth, and more metaphysics topics.

Shine lives in Sacramento, California.

instagram.com/_healingenergy_
tiktok.com/@shine_redwood

Fiction

THE MEDIUM, a short story, by Linda Westphal

A touching personal story about a resident of Savannah, Georgia, who is struggling to find a way to begin again after the unexpected death of her husband.

THE HERMIT BOOKSTORE, a novella, by Linda Westphal

On Tuesday the old farmhouse on Lotus Road is empty and locked, with a For Sale sign out front. On Wednesday of the same week, it's a charming used bookstore. How is this possible? That's the mystery Mary June, Mario, and Elisa have not been able to figure out.